Most Notable Elected Female Leaders

Debbie Nyman • Ricki Wortzman

Series Editor
Jeffrey D. Wilhelm

Much thought, debate, and research went into choosing and ranking the 10 items in each book in this series. We realize that everyone has his or her own opinion of what is most significant, revolutionary, amazing, deadly, and so on. As you read, you may agree with our choices, or you may be surprised — and that's the way it should be!

an imprint of
SCHOLASTIC

www.scholastic.com/librarypublishing

A Rubicon book published in association with Scholastic Inc.

 Rubicon © 2008 Rubicon Publishing Inc.
www.rubiconpublishing.com

All rights reserved. No part of this publication may be reproduced, stored in a database or retrieval system, distributed, or transmitted in any form or by any means, electronic, mechanical, photocopying, recording, or otherwise, without the prior written permission of Rubicon Publishing Inc.

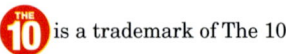 is a trademark of The 10 Books

SCHOLASTIC and associated logos and designs are trademarks and/or registered trademarks of Scholastic Inc.

Associate Publishers: Kim Koh, Miriam Bardswich
Project Editor: Amy Land
Editorial Assistant: Jessica Rose
Creative Director: Jennifer Drew
Project Manager/Designer: Jeanette MacLean
Graphic Designer: Rebecca Buchanan

The publisher gratefully acknowledges the following for permission to reprint copyrighted material in this book.

Every reasonable effort has been made to trace the owners of copyrighted material and to make due acknowledgment. Any errors or omissions drawn to our attention will be gladly rectified in future editions.

"Fighting for Freedom" from "Myanmar Dissident Marks 60th Birthday Under House Arrest" (excerpt). From the Canadian Broadcasting Corporation, June 20, 2005. Reprinted with Permission.

Reprinted by permission of KSG Alumni Bulletin, "Gro Harlem Brundtland: A Few Words from Madam Prime Minister" by Aine Cryts, Copyright 2004. President and Fellows of Harvard College. All rights reserved.

Cover: Margaret Thatcher–© Derek Hudson/Sygma/Corbis

Library and Archives Canada Cataloguing in Publication

Nyman, Debbie
  The 10 most notable elected female leaders / Debbie Nyman, Ricki Wortzman.

Includes index.
ISBN 978-1-55448-527-7

  1. Readers (Elementary). 2. Readers—Women. I. Wortzman, Ricki II. Title. III. Title: Ten most notable elected female leaders.

PE1117.N9527 2007a   428.6   C2007-906687-9

1 2 3 4 5 6 7 8 9 10   10   17 16 15 14 13 12 11 10 09 08

Printed in Singapore

Contents

Introduction: Women Who Rule! 4

Vigdís Finnbogadóttir 6
This remarkable leader worked tirelessly to promote the beauty and culture of her country.

Benazir Bhutto 10
This ex-prime minister hopes to bring democracy back to her country.

Ellen Johnson-Sirleaf 14
Being the first female leader of an African nation is not an easy task, especially in the war-torn country of Liberia.

Michelle Bachelet 18
You won't believe some of the challenges that Bachelet had to overcome before becoming the first female president of Chile.

Sirimavo Bandaranaike 22
After her husband was assassinated, Bandaranaike had no time to grieve — she took his place as prime minister.

Aung San Suu Kyi 26
Even while under house arrest, this fearless leader will not back down from her belief in freedom for Myanmar (Burma).

Golda Meir 30
This legendary leader was dedicated to establishing a safe and secure state.

Gro Harlem Brundtland 34
This notable leader dedicated her life to politics and continues to speak up for human rights and the environment.

Indira Gandhi 38
All leaders make sacrifices. But Indira Gandhi made the ultimate sacrifice — she gave her life for her country.

Margaret Thatcher 42
This "Iron Lady" wasn't just tough on issues such as the economy and war — she also brought environmental issues to her political platform.

We Thought … 46
What Do You Think? 47
Index 48

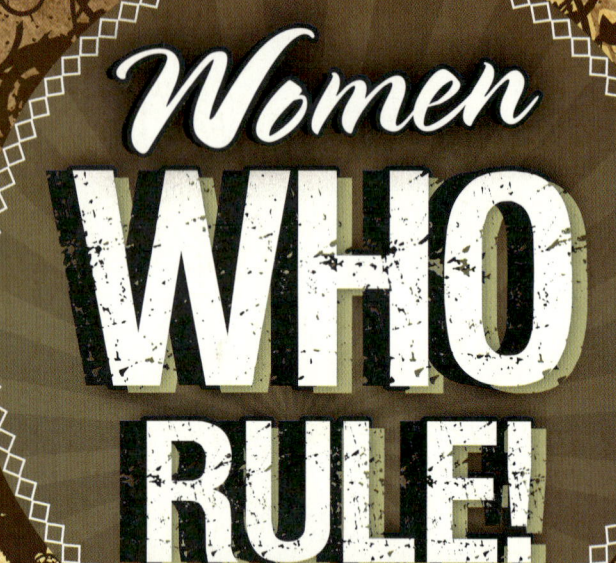
Women WHO RULE!

If you were elected the leader of your country, what changes would you make?

The elected female leaders in this book responded to this question in different ways. Sometimes people agreed with them and trusted their judgments. Other times, people disagreed with them and they were voted out of office, forced to leave their countries, or even assassinated.

These leaders believed they could make a difference. No matter how they entered the political arena, they pursued their political goals with courage, determination, and dedication. They carried out changes, and left a mark on their countries, and in many cases, the international community.

Vigdís Finnbogadóttir

ICELAND
Reykjavik
NORWAY
Oslo
UNITED KINGDOM
London

Margaret Thatcher

Ellen Johnson-Sirleaf

LIBERIA
Monrovia

CHILE
Santiago

Michelle Bachelet

To choose and rank the 10 female leaders in this book, we looked at obstacles and challenges they faced to get themselves elected. We also considered how they worked to create change and the impact they made in their countries and around the world. Finally, we took into account how powerful their countries were, because that could affect their influence on the world's stage. As you read about each of the leaders in this book, ask yourself:

What does it take to be a notable and influential ELECTED FEMALE LEADER?

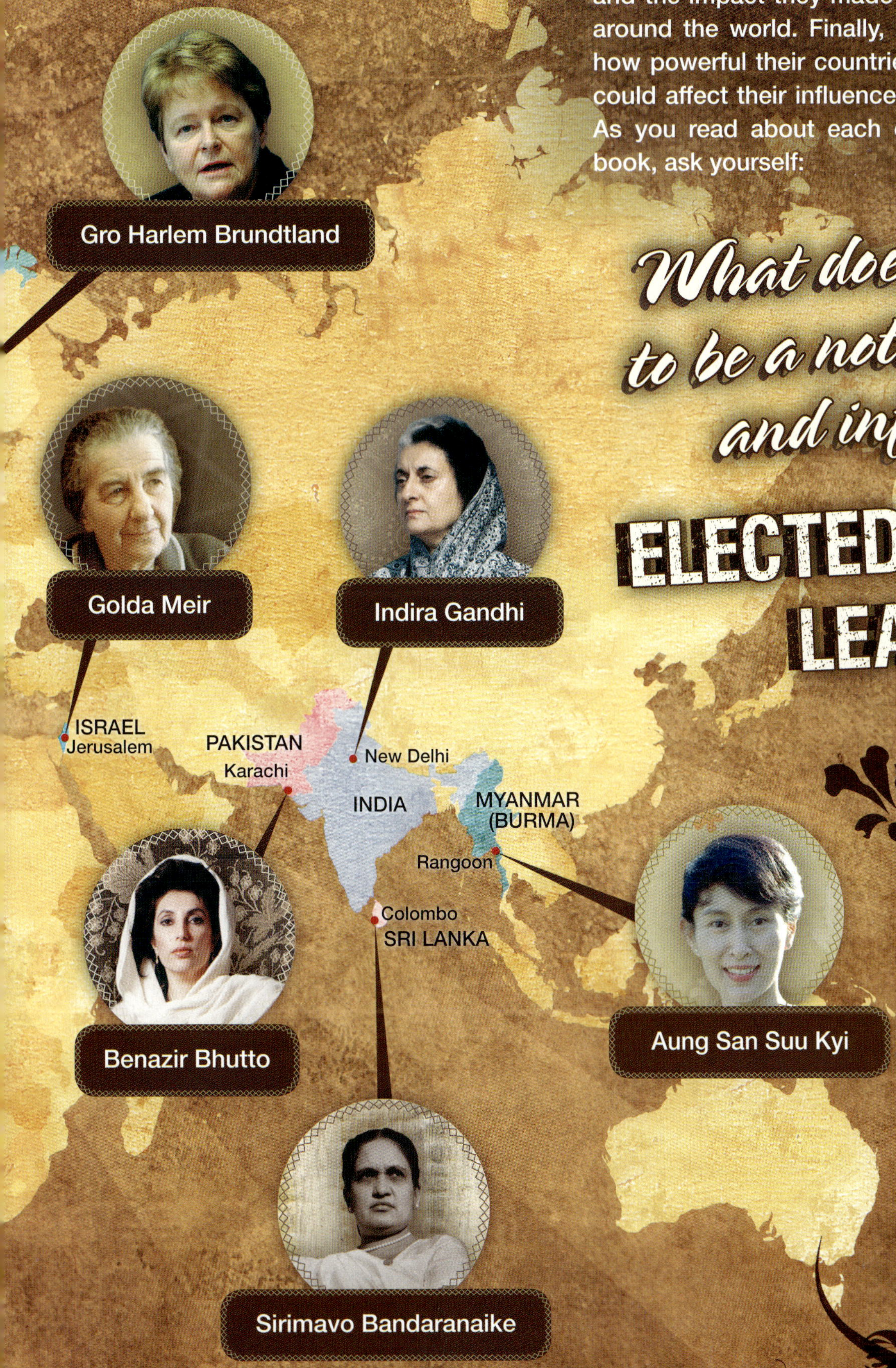

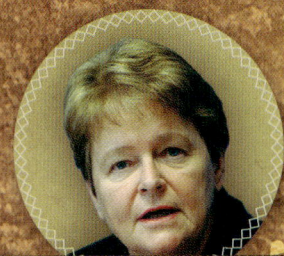

Gro Harlem Brundtland
Golda Meir
Indira Gandhi
ISRAEL
Jerusalem
PAKISTAN
Karachi
New Delhi
INDIA
MYANMAR
(BURMA)
Rangoon
Colombo
SRI LANKA
Benazir Bhutto
Aung San Suu Kyi
Sirimavo Bandaranaike

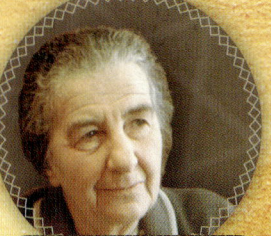

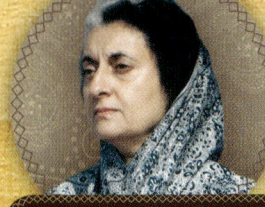

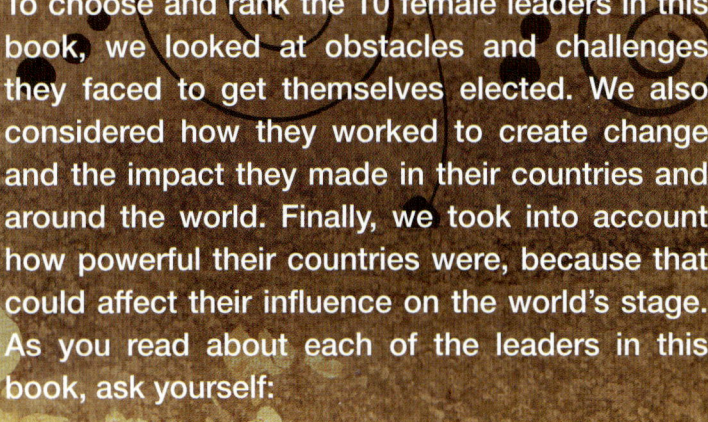

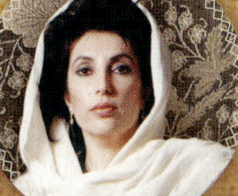

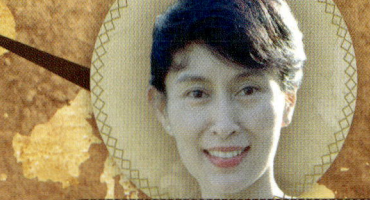

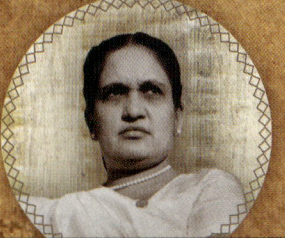

10 VIGDÍS FINNB

Vigdís Finnbogadóttir has said, "I don't want women to run the world alone, but if men and women could run the world together, things would be very different."

OGADÓTTIR

BIO: Born 1930 in Reykjavik, Iceland

ELECTED: President of Iceland from 1980 to 1996

Vigdís Finnbogadóttir (Vig-dees Fin-boh-guh-daw-ter) became a role model for every young woman in the world when she was elected president of Iceland in a national election on August 1, 1980. The people of Iceland, an island republic, boast that they were the first country to elect and then re-elect a woman as leader of their country. President Vigdís — Icelanders address their leaders by their first names — served her country as president for 16 years.

Iceland was once known as the land of the Vikings. Today, this small and unique island near the Arctic Circle is one of the wealthiest countries in the world and a favorite destination for tourists.

When her presidential terms were over in 1996, Finnbogadóttir took on a different role. In 1998, she was designated UNESCO's Goodwill Ambassador for Languages. Finnbogadóttir believes that understanding a country's language is a way to learn more about the people and their culture. She is committed to promoting diversity of languages, education, peace, and women's rights.

---

republic: *nation governed by officials who are voted into office by its people*
UNESCO: *United Nations Educational, Scientific and Cultural Organization*

VIGDÍS FINNBOGADÓTTIR

EARLY YEARS

Vigdís Finnbogadóttir learned the value of education and public service from her parents. Her father was a civil engineer and her mother was chair of the Icelandic Nurses Association for many years. Finnbogadóttir studied at universities in Iceland and France. She was a teacher and a director of the Reykjavik Theater Company before she turned to politics.

STATE OF THE NATION

When Finnbogadóttir took office, the position of president in Iceland was mainly ceremonial. She quickly changed that! In a land of limited natural resources, she knew that tourism was important. She thought that Iceland would be better known if she promoted the art and culture of the country. She supported Iceland's theaters and museums. Her cultural pursuits caught the attention of the world.

 Why do you think it is important for people to know about their cultural heritage? What would you want to preserve in your culture?

AT THE TOP

President Vigdís was a respected leader who made big changes. She actively promoted Nordic culture and was known for her outstanding work for the environment. She created reforestation programs to help stop Iceland from eroding into the sea. President Vigdís also reduced unfair hiring practices. This helped ensure equal rights for men and women in the workplace. She believes that "everything would be richer in flavor and color if more women participated."

Nordic: *of the region of Denmark, Finland, Iceland, Norway, and Sweden*
eroding: *wearing away caused by water, ice, or wind*

When Queen Elizabeth II visited, Finnbogadóttir showed her some little trees planted for her reforestation program. The queen said, "Yes, but where is the forest?" Vigdís replied, "Well, Your Majesty, with care and optimism some day it will be here."

Quick Fact
From the 13th century, Iceland was under the control of Norway and then Denmark. In 1819, Iceland became self-governing under Denmark. Iceland became an independent nation in 1944.

The Expert Says...

" Vigdís Finnbogadóttir ... was the first democratically elected woman in the world to serve as a president. During her 16 years as president ... children in Iceland grew up thinking only a woman could be president. "

— Barbara Palmer, journalist for *The Anniston Star*

10 9 8 7 6

Nordic Charm

During her terms in office, President Vigdís was passionate about putting Iceland on the map! These fact cards describe some issues that were important to her.

Tourism

Finnbogadóttir wanted to share the beauty of Iceland long before she was president. When she was young, she worked as a summer tour guide. Her job was to show international journalists around the country. As president, she actively promoted her country's art and culture to attract tourists from all over the world. She also paid close attention to environmental issues, ensuring that Iceland's mountains and glaciers would be around for generations to come.

Engaging Youth

Finnbogadóttir realized that young people often feel ignored by their leaders. During her 16 years as president, she worked closely with youth because she believed that they are the future of a country. She talked to them about issues like education and the environment. She hoped this would encourage them to grow up to be interested and active in the political world.

Art and Culture

In 1982, Vigdis Finnbogadóttir was part of a tour that brought Nordic art to America. It was called "Scandinavia Today." Leaders of the Nordic nations traveled to the United States to promote art and culture. Over a period of 15 months, Finnbogadóttir and the other leaders played an important role in events and exhibitions that featured Nordic music, fashion, photography, literature, and film. Many people learned about Icelandic art and culture from this art tour.

Quick Fact

Finnbogadóttir helped to set up the Council of Women World Leaders in 1996. This is a group made up of current and former female heads of government. Its goal is to inspire women to play an active role in politics.

 How does Finnbogadóttir's work at promoting art add to her image as a leader?

Take Note

President Vigdís is #10 on our list. She holds the distinction of being the world's first elected female president. She has made important changes to benefit her country and people, in particular women and youth. She has also made Iceland a presence on the world stage.
- Think of a few major changes that you would make in your country if you were elected leader of a country. How would you do this?

Quick Fact

Musician Yoko Ono chose Iceland to erect a peace tower to the realization of world peace. She unveiled the IMAGINE Peace Tower on October 9, 2007, saying, "I have chosen Iceland because it is a very unique eco-friendly country."

eco-friendly: *not harmful to the environment*

5 4 3 2 1

9 BENAZIR BH

Benazir Bhutto had to win her people's trust and confidence to show them that a woman could rule in a world usually governed by men.

UTTO

BIO: Born 1953 in Karachi, Pakistan

ELECTED: Prime minister of Pakistan for two terms: 1988–1990 and 1993–1996

Even as a child, Benazir Bhutto (Ben-uh-zeer Boo-toh) had big dreams. She had hopes of becoming a diplomat or journalist one day. But tragedy struck her family, and her future plans were changed forever.

Bhutto's father, Zulfikar Ali Bhutto, was president of Pakistan from 1971 to 1973, and prime minister from 1973 to 1977. The military took control of the country in 1977. They put Bhutto's father in prison and placed the family under house arrest. After her father was put to death in 1979, Bhutto spent the next seven years in prison in Pakistan and also in exile in England. But she promised to continue her father's fight for democracy.

In 1988, the leader of Pakistan's military died in a plane crash, and elections were held. Bhutto's party won, and she was elected the new prime minister. She became the first woman to lead the government of an Islamic state.

Bhutto credits her parents for her success, because she "was brought up to believe that a woman can do anything that a man can."

exile: *person who is forced out of his or her own country*
democracy: *political system where the people elect the government and have control over its power*

 Bhutto became the leader of her father's party after his death. Research other female leaders in history and compare their reasons for getting involved in politics.

BENAZIR BHUTTO

EARLY YEARS

Bhutto was encouraged by her father to become a strong, educated, and independent woman. She was educated at Harvard University in the United States and Oxford University in England. Her paternal grandfather, Sir Shah Nawaz Bhutto, was a key figure in Pakistan's independence movement. Pakistan became an independent country in 1947. Bhutto's father was leader of the People's Party and became president of Pakistan in 1971.

STATE OF THE NATION

Bhutto was only 35 when she was elected, making her the youngest woman ever to become the elected head of a government. The people of Pakistan had been ruled by the military for many years. Laws had been passed that denied women the rights to education and health care. Bhutto believed that the country needed to be more modern. To make this possible, she brought electricity to the countryside. She created schools to ensure that youth could grow up educated. She was also dedicated to improving conditions for women in Pakistan.

AT THE TOP

When she became prime minister, Bhutto wasted no time in creating economic and social programs. However, she was forced to leave office in 1990, after her government was accused of being corrupt. She was re-elected in 1993, but was again removed from power in 1996. As a result, her party did not follow through with its promises to pass legislation on health and equality issues. Bhutto left Pakistan in 1999 to escape charges of corruption.

> **?** Benazir Bhutto was placed under house arrest and has lived as an exile several times. How do you think this would change a person?

Pakistan People's Party activists hold photos of former Prime Minister Benazir Bhutto during a June 2007 protest in Karachi, Pakistan.

Exile

Like some of the other female leaders in this book, Benazir Bhutto knows what it is like to fall from power and live in exile. Read this article to learn more about Benazir Bhutto.

Benazir Bhutto is also known as the "Daughter of Pakistan." This is an interesting nickname for a woman who has spent many years of her life living outside of the country she loves.

She lived in exile before she was elected prime minister in 1988. She fled Pakistan again in 1999 when she and her husband were accused of mismanaging money, taking bribes, and giving jobs to people in her party when she was in power. Her husband was put in prison, but Bhutto escaped with her children. President Pervez Musharraf took control of Pakistan, returning the country to a state of military rule.

Bhutto was never convicted of the charges against her, and promised to return to Pakistan to restore democracy to the country.

Bhutto spent her years in exile living in London and Dubai. While in exile, Bhutto continued to work hard. She traveled around the world, speaking to world leaders about the need for democracy in Pakistan.

In 2007, Benazir Bhutto returned to Pakistan after eight years in exile. Thousands of people lined the streets to welcome her back. But the truck that she was traveling in was hit by explosives. Bhutto survived. However, about 150 people were killed and 200 were injured.

About the challenges she has faced, Bhutto once said: "The difference between somebody who succeeds and somebody who fails is the ability to absorb a setback."

The Expert Says...

" I write to let you know what a smashing success Benazir Bhutto's presentation to the sponsors of the World Affairs Council was ... Her empathy with the situation in the United States after September 11 and her positive outlook on relations between the Islamic and western world were a beacon of hope for all of us. "

— Wendell Fenton, President, World Affairs Council

Take Note

Benazir Bhutto ranks #9, ahead of President Vigdís. Bhutto has overcome personal tragedy and repeatedly shown the determination and courage to fight back and regain power. She refuses to give up her dream of bringing democracy back to Pakistan.

• What are the qualities that you would look for in a world leader? Make a list and rank them in order of importance.

8 ELLEN JOHNS

As Africa's first female president, Ellen Johnson-Sirleaf has worked tirelessly to help millions affected by Liberia's 14-year-long civil war.

ON-SIRLEAF

BIO: Born 1938 in Monrovia, Liberia

ELECTED: President of Liberia on January 16, 2006

Ellen Johnson-Sirleaf once said that she wanted to be president so that she could bring "emotion to the presidency." In January 2006, she got her wish. Johnson-Sirleaf was the first woman to be elected president of Liberia, a country on the west coast of Africa.

Liberia was the oldest republic in Africa. But in 1985, the government of the Republic of Liberia was overthrown by the military. The military government banned freedom of speech and elections. There was constant fighting among ethnic groups and tribes. This led to 14 years of civil war that destroyed Liberia's way of life and resulted in the deaths of many people. Johnson-Sirleaf was sentenced to 10 years in prison when she was charged with speaking out against the military. After a short period in jail, she left the country and continued her career abroad. When civil war ended in 2003, Johnson-Sirleaf moved back to Liberia. In 2005 she ran for president. She won, and took office in January of 2006.

Johnson-Sirleaf was nearly 70 years old when she was elected president of Liberia. She took on the challenge to run for office because of her dedication to bringing peace to Liberia. "Ma Ellen," as she is often called, is one remarkable woman!

 Is age a relevant consideration when choosing a leader? Why?

ELLEN JOHNSON-SIRLEAF

EARLY YEARS

Johnson-Sirleaf was born in Monrovia, the capital city of Liberia. Her family were Americo-Liberians. This means they were descendants of slaves from America who fled to Africa. They were often in social and political conflict with indigenous Liberians. After escaping her country during the military rule, she was educated at the best universities in the United States, where her commitment to social action took root. After her studies, she returned to Liberia and worked for the government in power.

STATE OF THE NATION

When Johnson-Sirleaf came to power, the countryside and towns were without electricity, water, and roads. Thousands of people had been left without homes, loved ones, and families. During the civil war, children had been forced to become soldiers. Her goal was to educate these children, to provide health care, reunite families, and rebuild the country. In 2006, she met with the U.S. Congress to ask for help to make her country "become a brilliant beacon, an example to Africa and the world of what love of liberty can achieve."

indigenous: *native*

? One of Johnson-Sirleaf's main tasks is to persuade people outside of Liberia to help her war-torn country. What can young people do to become involved with assisting Liberia?

AT THE TOP

In just over a year in office, Johnson-Sirleaf achieved many of her goals. She has established security and law enforcement agencies. She brought electricity and water to parts of the country, and rebuilt roads, bridges, and buildings with the help of UN peacekeepers and volunteers from around the world. With their help, she has built new homes for thousands of adults and children who were left homeless by the civil war. Johnson-Sirleaf has also built health clinics to help the sick. Most of all, she has brought hope to her people.

During the civil war, many Liberians were displaced and became refugees.

The Expert Says...

"Johnson-Sirleaf's courage and commitment to her country are an inspiration to me and women around the world."

— Laura Bush, First Lady of the United States

LOVE of LIBERTY

This is an excerpt of a speech that Ellen Johnson-Sirleaf delivered to the U.S. Congress on March 15, 2006. She outlines the need for aid to help the people of her country.

Ellen Johnson-Sirleaf

The national motto of Liberia — founded, as you know, by freed American slaves — is "The love of liberty brought us here." We became the first independent republic in Africa. Our capital, Monrovia, is named for your president James Monroe. … Our constitution and our laws were based upon yours. The U.S. dollar was long our legal tender and still is used alongside the Liberian dollar today. …

I came face to face with the human devastation of war, which killed a quarter of a million of our three million people and displaced most of the rest. … Our precious children died of malaria, parasites, and malnourishment. Our boys, full of potential, were forced to be child soldiers.

Former soldiers tell me they are tired of war; they do not want to have to fight or to run again. They want training. They want jobs. If they carry guns, they want to do so in defense of peace and security, not war and pillage. We must not betray their trust. …

[The people of Liberia] have the right to a government that is honest and that respects the sanctity of human life. They need and they deserve an economic environment in which their efforts can succeed. They need infrastructure and they need security. Above all, they need peace. That is the task of my administration. To meet that challenge, to do what is right, I ask for the continuing support of this Congress and the American people.

infrastructure: *a country's services and facilities, such as roads, power/water supplies, schools, hospitals, etc.)*

pillage: *looting; taking goods by force*

Quick Fact
Johnson-Sirleaf has received numerous international honors. These include the Grand Commander of the Star of African Redemption of Liberia (1980) and the Franklin D. Roosevelt Freedom of Speech Award from the United States (1988).

Take Note
To many, the work that needs to be done in Liberia seems overwhelming. Johnson-Sirleaf sees it is a challenge that calls for action. She recognizes that to bring change to Liberia she must form positive relationships with other African nations and express her vision to the world. For overcoming great odds and achieving success, she takes the #8 spot on our list.

- Find out about organizations that are active in developing and providing assistance to emerging African nations. What else do you think needs to be done?

5   4   3   2   1

7 MICHELLE BA

In her short time in office, Michelle Bachelet has paved the way for more Chilean women to hold positions in her government.

CHELET

BIO: Born 1951 in Santiago, Chile

ELECTED: President of Chile on March 11, 2006

Michelle Bachelet (Bash-e-let) is another leader who proves that it's possible to go from being a political prisoner to becoming the leader of a country.

In 1973, a military *coup* took place in Chile, a long and narrow country on the western coast of South America, between the Andes mountain range and the Pacific Ocean. The coup changed Bachelet's life forever. The military charged her father, who was a general in the army, with *treason*. They arrested and tortured him. After he died in prison, Bachelet and her mother were kidnapped and tortured. A relative pressured the military to release them. Both went into exile in 1975 and were allowed to return only in 1979. Bachelet continued with her medical studies, which were interrupted when she went into exile. She graduated as a doctor and worked to protect children of tortured and missing persons.

The military ruled Chile for 17 years. In 1990, democracy was restored. In 2005, Bachelet ran for election and won. She took control of the government in 2006 and became the first female president of Chile.

Bachelet has accomplished a lot in a short time. She is now even more popular with the public than before. This remarkable woman holds the #7 spot on our list.

coup: *sudden, violent takeover of government*
treason: *betraying one's country or government*

> **?** Torture, arrest, and exile did not stop Michelle Bachelet from standing up for her political beliefs. Compare how Bachelet and Bhutto got into politics.

MICHELLE BACHELET

EARLY YEARS

Bachelet's father served in the Chilean Air Force. As a child, she moved often because her father was posted to different military bases. Bachelet went to junior high in the United States where she learned to speak English fluently. She returned to Chile for high school and went on to medical school. Her education was interrupted when she went into exile, but she resumed her studies when she returned in 1979. After graduation, Bachelet went to work for the Ministry of Health. She then studied military strategy. Bachelet was appointed minister of health and then minister of defense. In 2005, she became a candidate for president.

> Michelle Bachelet is a leader in a male-dominated society. What challenges do you think a female leader would face in such a position?

STATE OF THE NATION

Shortly after she was elected, Bachelet faced her first crisis. Violence broke out in Chile, with hundreds of thousands of high-school students protesting the conditions of their education system. Bachelet used this opportunity to address issues that were important to the young people of the country. She was able to get them to return to class.

AT THE TOP

Bachelet promised reforms in the first 100 days of office, and successfully carried out most of them. She has created a cabinet with an equal number of men and women. She has made changes to reduce poverty and crime. She has also addressed the needs of youth by increasing the number of scholarships for students. In August 2006, she signed a free-trade agreement with China — Chile was the the first Latin American nation to do this.

cabinet: *group of government officials that help a leader make decisions*
free-trade: *buying and selling goods and services with no restriction*

The Expert Says...

" She's a very normal woman who has had a hard life, separated, bringing up children alone, experiencing real pain. These things bring her close to a society like [Chile's]. "

— Isabel Allende, member of Chilean congress

Quick Fact

In 2006, *Forbes* magazine ranked Michelle Bachelet as the 17th most powerful woman in the world. She reaches out to many countries by speaking their languages. She is fluent in Spanish, German, Portuguese, and French.

Michelle Bachelet greets Wu Bangguo of China to discuss free trade between the two countries.

IN THEIR OWN WORDS

These quotations offer us a glimpse of the new president of Chile and shed light on the significance of her political victory.

WHAT MICHELLE BACHELET SAYS ...

❝ Violence ravaged my life. I was a victim of hatred, and I have dedicated my life to reversing that hatred. ❞

ravaged: *destroyed; damaged*

❝ A president has to understand a country's needs. I am a mother and a doctor; I know the needs of my family and those of my country. ❞

❝ Today in Chile, one-third of households are run by women, we wake up, get the children ready, and go to work. To them I am hope. ❞

WHAT OTHERS SAY ...

❝ Bachelet's election is a manifestation of profound changes sweeping across Chilean society. ❞
— *Carolina Tohá, member of Chilean Congress*

❝ Bachelet is the first female president in South America to be elected strictly on her own merit and not as the wife of a 'great man.' ❞
— *Steve Anderson, director of the Santiago Times*

❝ She represents a new phenomenon in Chilean politics: the rise of a candidate from outside the male political elite. ❞
— *Roberto Espíndola, director of the Centre for European Studies at the University of Bradford, in the United Kingdom*

manifestation: *example; demonstration*
elite: *small group of people who are thought of as having the most power or influence*

Michelle Bachelet smiles to the public after her swearing-in ceremony.

Take Note

Torture, arrest, and exile did not stop Michelle Bachelet from standing up for her political beliefs. Showing courage, determination, and persistence, she has brought about significant changes. Her influence is felt in Chile, throughout Latin America, and around the world. She is #7 on our list.
• One of Bachelet's goals is to inspire women through example and legislation to take on positions of leadership. Do you think more women should be encouraged to take on leadership roles? Why?

6 SIRIMAVO BA

During her three terms in office, Sirimavo Bandaranaike moved Sri Lanka toward becoming an independent republic and helped to create a new constitution.

BANDARANAIKE

BIO: Born in Ratnapura, Ceylon (now Sri Lanka), 1916. Died in 2000.

ELECTED: Prime minister of Ceylon (Sri Lanka), holding office in 1960–1965, 1970–1977, and 1994–2000

Sometimes a tragic event can change a person's life forever. This was true for Sirimavo Bandaranaike (See-ree-mah-vaw Bahn-drah-nee-kee), the wife of the prime minister of Ceylon, now Sri Lanka, an island in the Indian Ocean just 28 miles from India.

When her husband was assassinated in 1959, Bandaranaike made a quick and unexpected entry into the political arena. Her husband's political party chose her to be its leader. She had no political experience, but Bandaranaike started to tour the country and make speeches. She was often called "weeping widow" as she would break into tears when she spoke of continuing her husband's work.

Bandaranaike won the national election in 1960. She became the world's first woman prime minister. She then served as prime minister in the 1960s and '70s, fell from power in the '80s, and regained it in the '90s and 2000s. While she was prime minister, Sri Lanka became a republic, independent from British rule. Bandaranaike died at the age of 84 from a heart attack while she was on her way home after voting in the country's general election.

? Bandaranaike mourned her husband's death in public instead of only in private. Do you think this affected how she was seen as a leader?

SIRIMAVO BANDARANAIKE

EARLY YEARS

As a child, Bandaranaike never dreamed of becoming a politician. But this doesn't mean that she wasn't a strong and independent woman. She was active in many social programs. She visited villages to teach crafts, and spoke about the need for equal rights and education for women.

STATE OF THE NATION

Upon taking power in 1960, Bandaranaike changed Sri Lanka's official language from English to Sinhalese. This was the language spoken by the Sinhalese majority in the country. The Tamil population felt left out because they were a group of people who spoke a different language. It became more difficult for them to access government positions as well as the legal system. Tension between the two groups led to a civil war in 1983. Despite this trouble at home, Bandaranaike was able to strengthen Sri Lanka's role internationally. She did so by forming ties with China, India, and Pakistan.

Quick Fact

The civil war in Sri Lanka was fought between two ethnic groups, the majority Sinhalese and the Tamils. The Tamils felt they were discriminated over language, accessibility to education, and other human rights issues. A group called the Liberation Tigers of Tamil Eelam started the war in 1983. Tens of thousands were killed in the violent struggle. Although a ceasefire was reached in 2003, tension still simmers to this day.

AT THE TOP

As prime minister, Bandaranaike placed the banking and insurance companies under government control. During her second term as prime minister, her government introduced a new constitution to cut ties with Great Britain. Ceylon was renamed the Republic of Sri Lanka. Though her policies and actions were often criticized at home, she changed the way the world viewed her country. She ended her years as prime minister respected more abroad than at home. In 1994, she became prime minister for the third time. This time she was appointed by her daughter, who was the president of the country.

? Bandaranaike made decisions that were not popular with the Tamil community. Think about an important decision you have made. What did you take into consideration? Do you think it was a good decision? Why?

Sirimavo Bandaranaike, with her daughter, Chandrika, in July 1964.

IT RUNS IN THE FAMILY

Sirimavo Bandaranaike controlled politics in Sri Lanka for more than four decades. Like it or not, she was an influential figure in her country's history. So were her husband and three children, as shown in these profiles.

SOLOMON BANDARANAIKE

Solomon, Sirimavo Bandaranaike's husband, came from a well-to-do Sinhalese family. A lawyer by training, he was active in politics. He became prime minister in 1956. He was assassinated in 1959.

CHANDRIKA KUMARATUNGA

The younger daughter of Solomon and Sirimavo was only 14 when her father was killed. In 1989, another tragedy struck — her husband was gunned down. Kumaratunga had her mother's support to pursue a political career. She was elected president in 1994 and 2000. Her term expired in 2005, and the law did not allow her to run again.

SUNETHRA BANDARANAIKE

The family's elder daughter worked in the women's movement of her mother's party. She also helped to campaign for her mother. But politics was clearly not her interest. In 1994, she devoted her time to helping young and talented artists. Today, she runs the Sunera Foundation, an organization that provides dance and drama training to help disabled youth build confidence.

ANURA BANDARANAIKE

Sirimavo's son, Anura, never became the president or prime minister of Sri Lanka, but he served in different positions in the government of Sri Lanka. He was in his family's political party for much of his political life.

The Expert Says...

" After her husband died, there was so much confusion and the party was almost collapsing. She was an untried leader. But she not only survived, she **sustained** the party and the family in politics. "

— K. M. de Silva, Sri Lankan historian

sustained: *strengthened; supported*

? What do you think were some major challenges that faced Bandaranaike when she entered politics suddenly and without much preparation?

Take Note

Sirimavo Bandaranaike is #6 on our list. Like Michelle Bachelet, she entered into politics because of a family tragedy. She had to make tough decisions under challenging and dangerous circumstances. She was devoted to the politics of her country, and played an active role until her death.

- Solomon and Sirimavo Bandaranaike were both prime ministers and their daughter Chandrika Kumaratunga was president. Do you think it is a good idea for children to follow in their parents' footsteps? Using politics as an example, or any other career, explain the advantages and disadvantages.

5 AUNG SAN SUU

Aung San Suu Kyi's party was elected in 1990, but the government in power refused to hand her the leadership. She now lives under house arrest where she continues to fight for democracy in Myanmar.

KYI

BIO: Born 1945 in Rangoon, Burma (now Myanmar)

ELECTED: Prime minister of Myanmar in May 1990, but when the country's military regime would not recognize her party's victory, she was not allowed to take office.

Imagine that you are standing in front of a group of armed soldiers who tell you they will shoot if you take another step. Imagine taking that step! Unarmed and staring the soldiers in the eye, Aung San Suu Kyi (Awng Sahn Soo Chee) took the step and kept walking! She has continued to take steps against her country's violent military regime.

Myanmar is located in southeastern Asia and borders the Andaman Sea and the Bay of Bengal. The country gained independence from Britain in 1948 and became a democratic republic until the military seized control in 1960.

The people of Myanmar suffered under military rule, and the country was in economic decline. In 1988, the people took to the streets in protest against the government. For speaking out against the military, Suu Kyi was put under house arrest. Thousands of protestors were killed, but the people continued their fight for democracy. In 1990, the military regime was forced to call an election. Suu Kyi's political party won a landslide victory.

regime: *ruling government*

? Aung San Suu Kyi said, "It is not power that corrupts but fear. Fear of losing power corrupts those who willed it." What do you think she means? Do you agree and why?

AUNG SAN SUU KYI

EARLY YEARS

Aung San Suu Kyi was only two years old when her father, General Aung San, was assassinated in 1947. He had led the fight for Burma's independence from Great Britain. Burma was established as an independent republic in 1948, one year after his death. Suu Kyi followed in her father's footsteps, fighting against the military regime that put an end to democracy in Burma. In 1988, her life took a new turn when she returned to Burma after studying abroad. She was home during one of the largest uprisings in the country's history.

STATE OF THE NATION

Myanmar, one of the poorest countries in the world, is known for its harsh regime. A strong military governs the country and instills fear in the people. In 1988, Suu Kyi gave her first political speech. Several hundred thousand people were there to listen. Soon, the military banned all political gatherings of more than four people. Suu Kyi ignored this ban. She traveled across the country to give speeches. She helped to create a political party called the National League for Democracy.

In 1990, her party won the election by capturing an impressive 82 percent of the seats in parliament. But the military refused to recognize the results and Suu Kyi is still under house arrest today.

AT THE TOP

The international community has recognized Suu Kyi's struggles for freedom. In 1991, she was awarded the Nobel Peace Prize for her nonviolent struggle for democracy and human rights." She used the $1.3 million prize to create education and health programs. Her nonviolent protests include writing books, educating people around the world about the need for democracy, and discouraging tourists from visiting her country.

Her freedom is still restricted. When her husband died in London, she could not attend his funeral. House arrest, travel restrictions, and detentions continue to be part of Suu Kyi's life. She is unable to see her children or any other family members who live outside of Myanmar.

? What does the example of Suu Kyi tell you about standing up and fighting for a cause?

Aung San Suu Kyi poses with an image of her father, General Aung San.

The Expert Says...

" In the good fight for peace ... we are dependent on persons who set examples, persons who can symbolize what we are seeking and mobilize the best in us. Aung San Suu Kyi is just such a person. "

— Francis Sejersted, chair of the Nobel Peace Prize Committee

Quick Fact

During the uprising in 1988, the military killed up to 10,000 demonstrators. In 1989, it changed the name of Burma to Myanmar. Many people still protest this change because recognizing the name would mean accepting the military's decision and power.

FIGHTING FOR FREEDOM

SUU KYI MARKS 60TH BIRTHDAY UNDER HOUSE ARREST

An article from CBC News, June 20, 2005

... Several hundred supporters met at the offices of [Suu Kyi's] National League for Democracy party with several foreign diplomats to applaud the release of 10 doves and 61 balloons. They marked the 10 years she has been locked up and the start to her 61st year.

A separate group of about 12 party members wearing T-shirts with her photo above the phrase "Set her free" released another flock of 61 doves at a downtown temple.

Police detained them until they removed the shirts.

"Religious ceremonies and other quiet ceremonies are being held all over the country," Nan Khin Htwe Myint, a 68-year-old party official, said.

But elsewhere in the country, which has been ruled by the military since 1962, supporters were warned not to celebrate the Nobel Peace Prize laureate's birthday.

laureate: *winner of an award*

Members of the National League for Democracy party hold signs protesting Aung San Suu Kyi's house arrest.

Suu Kyi is confined under tight security to a run-down house with a front yard overgrown like a jungle. She is believed to be in good health, but her only visitors are a woman who cooks and her daughter. Doctors have not visited since last year. ...

Take Note

Suu Kyi takes the #5 spot. She has not been allowed to assume her office as prime minister, but she is an inspiration to her people. Her nonviolent protest against an oppressive regime is an example of courage that inspires people around the world.
- How would you introduce Aung San Suu Kyi to a gathering of people? Think of all the words you can use to describe her personal sacrifices, her suffering, and her character.

4 GOLDA MEIR

Golda Meir had a grandmotherly image, but her people also referred to her as the "Iron Lady."

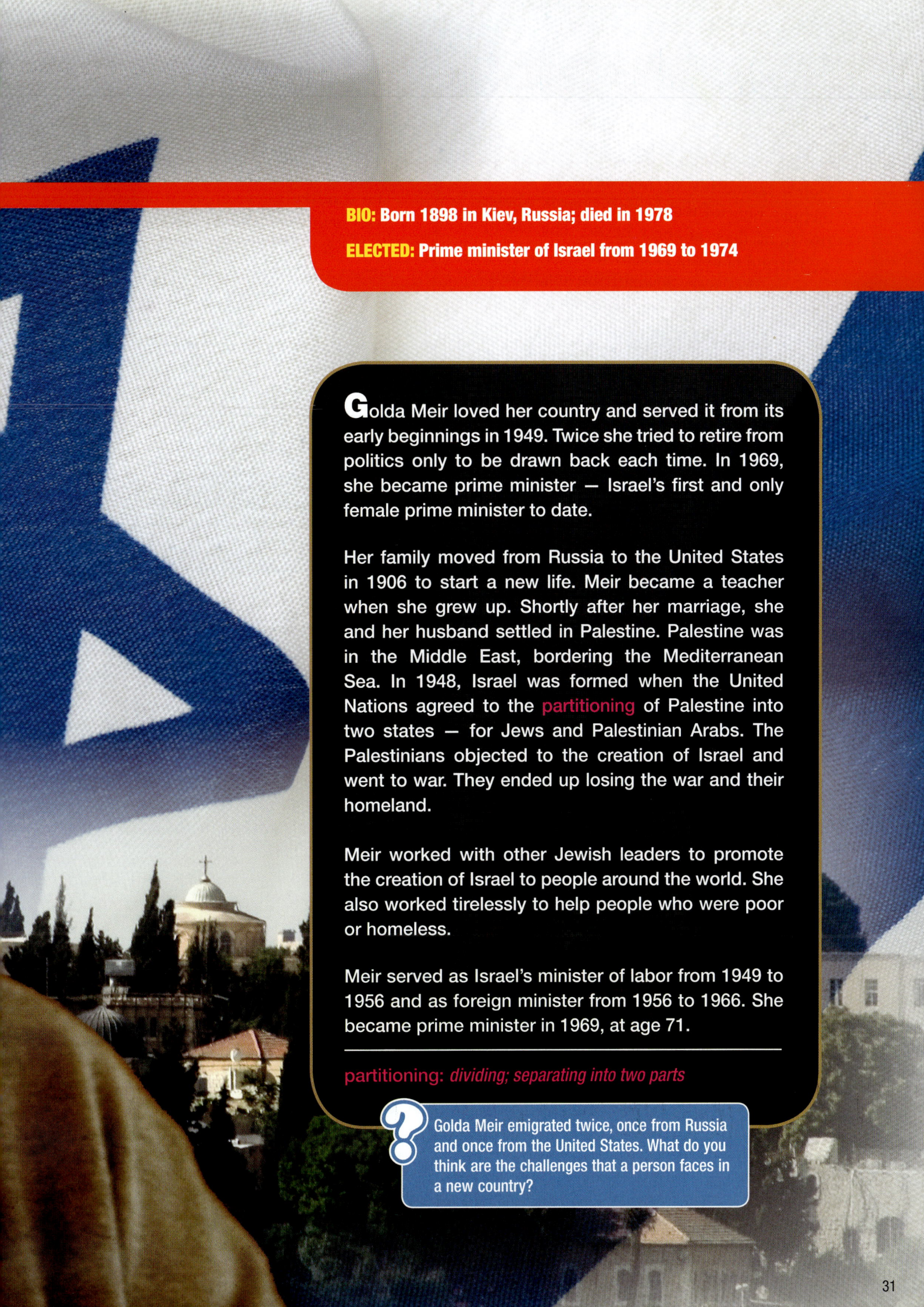

BIO: Born 1898 in Kiev, Russia; died in 1978

ELECTED: Prime minister of Israel from 1969 to 1974

Golda Meir loved her country and served it from its early beginnings in 1949. Twice she tried to retire from politics only to be drawn back each time. In 1969, she became prime minister — Israel's first and only female prime minister to date.

Her family moved from Russia to the United States in 1906 to start a new life. Meir became a teacher when she grew up. Shortly after her marriage, she and her husband settled in Palestine. Palestine was in the Middle East, bordering the Mediterranean Sea. In 1948, Israel was formed when the United Nations agreed to the **partitioning** of Palestine into two states — for Jews and Palestinian Arabs. The Palestinians objected to the creation of Israel and went to war. They ended up losing the war and their homeland.

Meir worked with other Jewish leaders to promote the creation of Israel to people around the world. She also worked tirelessly to help people who were poor or homeless.

Meir served as Israel's minister of labor from 1949 to 1956 and as foreign minister from 1956 to 1966. She became prime minister in 1969, at age 71.

partitioning: *dividing; separating into two parts*

? Golda Meir emigrated twice, once from Russia and once from the United States. What do you think are the challenges that a person faces in a new country?

GOLDA MEIR

EARLY YEARS

Meir's memories of her days in Russia include her father nailing boards across the front door of their house. The family was afraid of being forced out of their home because they were Jewish. She fought hard all her life to make sure her people would live in a country without fear.

STATE OF THE NATION

When Meir became prime minister, Israel was poor, but confident and nationalistic. The country never enjoyed peace with its Arab neighbors and security was always a challenge. Meir faced a crisis in 1972, when Israeli athletes were taken hostage during the Olympic Games in Munich, Germany. She was criticized by some for not doing more to negotiate with the hostage-takers. In the end, 11 athletes were killed. In 1973, Israel was attacked by neighboring Arab states and Egypt. This proved to be the hardest time in her political life.

> **?** Meir refused to negotiate with people who used violence, kidnapping, and threats. Do you agree with her decision? Why or why not?

AT THE TOP

Meir led her country with passion and commitment. She encouraged Jewish people from all over the world to move to Israel. She forged relations with the United States and other nations to bring foreign aid to the country. Meir gained a reputation as a tough and effective leader. Her greatest challenge was the territorial conflict between Israel and Arab countries. Meir was criticized for her refusal to recognize the Palestinian people and their quest for a homeland. She pursued a firm policy but was always hopeful for a peaceful solution.

nationalistic: *extremely patriotic*

Like other Israeli leaders, Golda changed her last name to have a Hebrew name. Meir means "one who shines."

Quick Fact
Golda Meir's life has inspired writers to write books, movies, and plays to tell her story. These include the play *Golda's Balcony* and a television miniseries entitled *A Woman Named Golda*.

The Expert Says...
" Golda Meir is a woman one cannot help but deeply respect and deeply love. "
— Eleanor Roosevelt, former First Lady of the United States

Golda Meir

*This **timeline** traces the accomplishments of a dedicated political leader.*

1928 Assumes her first political position, as the secretary of the Women's Labor Council.

1930 Helps to found the Labor Party of the Land of Israel.

1948 Signs the official document to declare the founding of Israel.

1949 Wins election to Israel's parliament. She becomes the minister of labor, focusing on immigration and housing. She remains in this position until 1956.

1956 Becomes Israel's foreign minister.

1965 Declines an offer to become deputy prime minister for health reasons.

1966 Leaves her position as foreign minister and becomes secretary-general of her party.

1969 Becomes prime minister after the death of Levi Eshkol.

1974 Retires from politics because of her failing health.

1978 Dies in December at the age of 80.

Quick Fact

Egypt was the first Muslim country to sign a peace treaty with Israel in 1979. Jordan followed in 1994. Israel has not signed final peace agreements with Syria or with the Palestiine Liberation Organization (PLO), which represents the Palestinian people.

Take Note

Golda Meir is ranked #4 on our list. Her influence was felt far beyond the borders of Israel. She was not afraid to go to war to defend her country. She created relationships with foreign countries and brought much needed resources and funds to Israel. She had a huge impact on Jewish people living throughout the world, encouraging many of them to settle in Israel.
- Think of a time in your life when you had to take action to get something done for your family or community. Did you succeed? Explain.

5　　4　　3　　2　　1

③ GRO HARLEM

Brundtland is a pioneer in the movement to stop climate change. More than 20 years ago, she wrote an important report called "Our Common Future." It talked about important environmental issues and the need for change.

BRUNDTLAND

BIO: Born 1939 in Oslo, Norway

ELECTED: Prime minister of Norway, holding office in 1981, 1986–1989, and 1990–1996

From a young age, Gro Harlem Brundtland (Gro Harlem Broont-land) loved to talk about politics with her family. At the age of seven, she was already in the youth division of her father's political party. Brundtland grew up to become the party's leader and the first female prime minister of Norway, a country on the Arctic Ocean bordered by Finland, Sweden, and Russia.

Brundtland shared her father's interests in politics and medicine. After completing her medical studies, she went on to study public health. She worked for the Oslo Board of Health from 1968 to 1974. Then she was appointed minister of the environment. In 1981, she took over the office of the prime minister for a year. This made her not only the first female prime minister but also the youngest. Her government lost power, but five years later she ran in the election and won.

A born leader, Brundtland has made a mark in her country and in the international community. She has fought for the rights of women and children. She has worked to reduce poverty and disease. She has won numerous awards for her work in public health and the environment.

 Think of a person who has inspired you. What do you admire most about this person?

GRO HARLEM BRUNDTLAND

EARLY YEARS

Brundtland's father was a doctor who became a politician. From an early age, her family encouraged her to discuss politics and to ask questions. It was no surprise, therefore, that Brundtland went on to pursue a career in public health and politics!

STATE OF THE NATION

As minister of the environment, Brundtland was committed to preserving the natural beauty of Norway. She wrote many articles on environmental issues, such as the threat of pollution, and raised the awareness of the international community to this problem. When she was prime minister, the question of whether Norway should join the European Union was discussed throughout Europe. Brundtland urged her people to become part of the European Union, but they voted against it in 1994. This proved to be the biggest defeat of her government.

European Union: *economic and political association of countries in Europe that began in 1993, sharing a common currency — the euro*

AT THE TOP

Brundtland is a strong supporter of women's rights. She adopted a policy to ensure that women made up 40 percent of her government. She worked tirelessly to ensure that females had access to education and equal-paying jobs, and created programs to help the jobless. This resulted in an extremely low unemployment rate in Norway. In 1983, Brundtland became head of the World Commission on Environment and Development. She called on governments to protect the environment.

? Norway has the highest percentage of women in top government positions in the world. Do you think your government has done enough to support women in politics? Explain your answer.

Brundtland tried to reduce greenhouse gases in Norway by creating a carbon dioxide tax in 1990. This meant raising the price of fuel, which creates carbon dioxide.

Quick Fact

In 1998, Brundtland received international recognition when she was elected as the first female Director-General of the World Health Organization. This branch of the United Nations is responsible for promoting worldwide health, especially in poor countries.

The Expert Says…

"Few have dedicated more of their career to advancing the understanding of the … relationship between politics and public health than Dr. Gro Harlem Brundtland. She has devoted her lifework to persuading world leaders to take science seriously."

— Heather Holliday, journalist at the University of California, San Diego

Life in Politics

Find out what Prime Minister Gro Harlem Brundtland has to say in this interview.

Q You've written a memoir of your life in politics. ... What did you want to share with readers about your life?

A The process allowed me to slow down and take a look at the course of my life. When you've spent so many years of your life [being] so busy, you don't have the time to do that. I also wanted to have a chance to tell readers about my life from my perspective.

Q Do you consider yourself an optimist?

A Yes, I do. I think optimism is a requirement for a leader. You have to believe that you can change things. You can't just sit there and say that something doesn't work. You have to believe that you can make change happen, and you have to be able to communicate that to others. That's what leadership is all about.

Q Do you think that women in leadership roles are different from their male counterparts?

A I think that humanity would be denied the talents of women if women weren't in leadership positions. But I should say that, while women tend to be better listeners, there are women who aren't great listeners and men who are great listeners. And some women are great at engaging in conversation, while others are not. My point is that all women don't bring the same qualities to their roles as leaders. All women aren't the same and all men aren't the same.

? What would be your first question for Gro Harlem Brundtland if you had a chance to interview her?

Take Note

As a leader, Brundtland carried out important changes in her country in the areas of public health and women's rights. Her influence on issues of the environment, public health, and equality for women reached the international community. Brundtland's reputation as a leader has earned her the #3 spot on our list.

• Compare the leadership and achievements of Brundtland and another leader you have read about so far. In what ways are they different or similar?

5   4   **3**   2   1

② INDIRA GAN[DHI]

Indira Gandhi was voted the greatest woman of the past 1,000 years in a poll by the British Broadcasting Corporation. The runners-up were Queen Elizabeth II and Mother Teresa.

DHI

BIO: Born 1917 in Allahabad, India; assassinated in New Delhi, India, on October 31, 1984

ELECTED: Prime minister of India: 1966–1977 and 1980–1984

Indira Gandhi (In-deer-uh Gahn-dee) was first elected to India's parliament in 1964. Two years later, she was the first female prime minister of India. She was born into India's most powerful political family. Her grandfather was a leader in the movement for India's independence. Her father was prime minister of India for 17 years.

Indira Gandhi was a shy person. She did not enjoy the public life of a politician, but she had a strong sense of duty. After the death of her mother, she managed her father's official residence while he was prime minister.

Throughout her years in public life, she worked very hard. She proved to be a tough and wise leader. Her term in office was cut short in 1984. She was assassinated by her trusted bodyguards.

Today, Indira Gandhi is remembered as one of the most influential figures in India's history.

? Indira Gandhi was born into India's most powerful political family. How would this be an advantage or disadvantage to her political career?

INDIRA GANDHI

EARLY YEARS

Indira Gandhi's grandfather and father were influential politicians. She came to know many of their important friends. She became involved in politics at an early age. At 12, she was the leader of the Monkey Brigade, a group of children who sang songs, made speeches, and organized marches to support the fight for India's independence from Great Britain.

STATE OF THE NATION

When Gandhi was prime minister, India had a population of nearly 700 million. There were growing conflicts because of food shortages, unemployment, and poverty. In 1971, there was a civil war between East and West Pakistan. India helped East Pakistan defeat West Pakistan. After the war, East Pakistan became Bangladesh, and India became a war power with military support from the Soviet Union. Gandhi had to deal with political opponents and unrest among religious groups.

AT THE TOP

Gandhi created assistance programs and improved the living conditions of her people. She created jobs in science and technology, and built a strong army. In 1974, India completed a successful underground nuclear test. At first, people loved her. But in 1975, she was charged with breaking election rules. When she decided not to step down, violence broke out. She had the leaders of the opposition arrested. In 1977, Gandhi was voted out of office. She made a comeback three years later. She was re-elected as prime minister.

Quick Fact

In June 1984, Gandhi sent Indian troops to the Punjab to stop growing conflict. The troops stormed into a Sikh temple. This angered many people and led to violence. More than 600 people were killed. This action cost Gandhi her life. In October 1984, she was killed by her trusted Sikh bodyguards.

The Expert Says...

"If the list of Indira's faults and flaws is long, that of her achievements, some of them dazzling, is even longer and more impressive."

— Inder Malhotra, author of *Indira Gandhi: A Personal and Political Biography*

At a political rally the night before Indira Gandhi was assassinated, she said to the crowd, "I don't mind if my life goes in the service of the nation. If I die today, every drop of my blood will invigorate the nation."

This 1927 family portrait shows a young Indira Gandhi (second from right) and her father Jawaharlal Nehru (top left).

A Political Dynasty

Indira Gandhi's family tree features some of the most influential leaders in India's politics. Check out their profiles below.

Motilal Nehru (1861–1931)
Gandhi's Grandfather

He was the head of a political family that produced three prime ministers. A lawyer by profession, he became the leader of the Indian National Congress, which was India's biggest political party. He raised awareness for independence.

Jawaharlal Nehru (1889–1964)
Gandhi's Father

He was one of the youngest leaders of the Indian National Congress. He became the first prime minister of India after it achieved independence from Britain. He introduced industries and land reforms, and created programs to improve education and welfare. He was popular and well respected.

Indira Gandhi

Rajiv Gandhi (1944–1991)
Gandhi's First Son

He was sworn in as prime minister shortly after Indira Gandhi was assassinated. In 1984, he won the election by a big margin. He was the youngest prime minister in India's history. A suicide bomber killed him in 1991.

Sanjay Gandhi (1946–1980)
Gandhi's Second Son

He was elected to the parliament of India in 1980. His political life was cut short when he died in an airplane crash only five months later.

Sonia Gandhi (1946 –)
Gandhi's Daughter-in-Law

She is now president of the Indian National Congress, the fifth member of the Nehru family to hold the position. She declined the job of prime minister after her party won the elections in 2004. She is recognized as one of the most powerful women in the world today.

? Think of another influential political family in history. What impact did they have in the politics of their country?

Take Note

Indira Gandhi is #2 on our list. She was elected to lead one of the world's largest nations, not once but twice. With a population the size of India, there were many social and political challenges. Gandhi made some unpopular choices, but she proved to be a strong and influential leader.
- Think of a decision or a choice you made that proved unpopular with your friends or family. What made you do it and why?

2

1 MARGARET

Besides being a great public speaker, Margaret Thatcher is a talented writer. She is the author of five books including The Collected Speeches and Statecraft: Strategies for a Changing World.

THATCHER

BIO: Born 1925 in Lincolnshire, England

ELECTED: Prime minister of the United Kingdom of Great Britain and Northern Ireland from 1979 to 1990

Margaret Thatcher was the first female prime minister of the United Kingdom. She was elected to three successive terms in office and served as prime minister for 11 years. This is longer than any other prime minister in the United Kingdom in the 20th century.

Thatcher came from a working-class background and rose to power on her own merit. She believed that everyone could become successful through hard work and perseverance. Once elected, Thatcher took immediate steps to improve the economy. She introduced policies that were not popular with everyone. She reduced the power of the unions and cut back on public spending. The world saw her as a strong and influential leader. She was against communism and played an important role in helping to end the Cold War. In 1982, she scored a major victory with her people when she sent troops to war in the Falkland Islands to protect British interests.

Thatcher became known as the "Iron Lady." She was a stern leader who could make difficult decisions. But she was also criticized for her economic policies in the late 1980s. She resigned from office in 1990.

successive: *following one another without gaps*
Cold War: *political rivalry that existed between the Soviet Union and the United States after World War II*

MARGARET THATCHER

EARLY YEARS

She was born Margaret Hilda Roberts and came from humble beginnings. Her father was a grocer in a small town. Thatcher studied at Oxford University and earned two degrees, one in chemistry and another in law. In 1950, she was the youngest woman to run for parliament. She lost, but she did not give up. She eventually became a member of Parliament in 1959.

Quick Fact
In 2002, Thatcher had a stroke that has impaired her memory. However, this hasn't stopped her. She continues to be visible in the public eye, giving speeches and attending ceremonies.

STATE OF THE NATION

Thatcher came into power when prices were rising and many people were out of work. She had to deal with strikes by workers across the country. She also had to face the ongoing conflict with the IRA (Irish Republican Army) who wanted to free Northern Ireland from British rule. In 1982, Thatcher faced a major challenge when Argentina's military invaded the Falkland Islands, a British territory. Thatcher made a tough decision. She sent the navy to recapture the Falkland Islands.

> In 1984, Thatcher escaped injury when a bomb exploded in the hotel where she was staying. What are the hazards of the job of a politician? What are the rewards?

AT THE TOP

Margaret Thatcher made bold and sometimes unpopular moves. But the economy prospered and unemployment dropped. Her popularity rose when the United Kingdom won the Falklands War against Argentina and brought about a wave of patriotism and national pride. Her openness to meet and negotiate with the Soviet Premier Gorbachev influenced President Reagan to reconsider the Cold War. Thatcher was credited with playing an important role in ending the Cold War between the two countries.

> What factors, besides winning a war, can help to build patriotism in a country?

Margaret Thatcher stands with Prince Charles (far left) and a Falklands military commander at a ceremony commemorating the 25th anniversary of the end of the Falklands War.

The Expert Says...

" The prime ministers who are remembered are those who think and teach, and not many do. Mrs. Thatcher ... influenced the thinking of a generation. "

— Tony Benn, as quoted in *The Prime Minister: The Job and Its Holders Since 1945* by Peter Hennessy

Margaret Thatcher, 1977

What It Takes

In the following **quotations**, Margaret Thatcher reveals what it takes to be a good leader.

"I just owe almost everything to my father and it's passionately interesting for me that the things that I learned in a small town, in a very modest home, are just the things that I believe have won the election."

"I do not know anyone who has got to the top without hard work. That is the recipe. It will not always get you to the top, but should get you pretty near."

"Disciplining yourself to do what you know is right and important, although difficult, is the high road to pride, self-esteem, and personal satisfaction."

"If you lead a country like Britain, a strong country, a country which has taken a lead in world affairs in good times and in bad, a country that is always reliable, then you have to have a touch of iron about you."

"I love argument; I love debate. I don't expect anyone just to sit there and agree with me; that's not their job."

Take Note

During her terms in office, Thatcher led her country to war overseas, faced challenges of political unrest, survived an attempted assassination, and created an economic policy that was loved by some but hated by others. She was also seen as a significant force in ending the Cold War between the Soviet Union and the United States. For playing a key role in shaping her country and the world, Thatcher has our vote for the #1 spot on our list.

- Compare Margaret Thatcher and Indira Gandhi. Use the following headings: Family Background, Education, Leadership Style, Challenges, and Accomplishments. Who would you choose as the top most notable female leader? Why?

We Thought …

Here are the criteria we used in ranking the 10 most notable female leaders.

These women:
- Had the dedication and desire to serve their country
- Used their platforms to create change
- Overcame great personal and political challenges
- Broke the barriers that existed in their countries
- Changed the way people around the world viewed their country
- Fought for human rights, including rights for women, children, and the poor
- Had a lasting impression and touched the lives of millions
- Made great personal sacrifices to become a leader
- Inspired others to fight for change